The Mini-Book on

Use Cases

All you need, but short

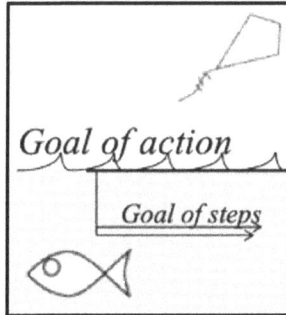

Alistair Cockburn

The Simplifying Series

What a fantastic breakdown of the art of crafting effective use cases! I found this especially helpful for aligning cross-functional teams swiftly, especially when time is of the essence.

-- Agile Luminary

Cockburn's clarity cuts through complexity - this is a must-read for any Agile team serious about building what users actually need, not just what specs say.

-- Jawahar Prabhu Yenneti

So much business writing feels bloated, but this cuts straight to the signal. Clear, crisp, and immediately applicable. I'm building out foundational education tools for my consulting practice, and your book is helping me shape how I introduce use case thinking to clients. Thanks for making this both accessible and deeply useful.

-- Richard Crazythunder, Founder, Celatum Origin

ISBN 979-8-9985862-3-1 for paper,
ISBN 979-8-9985862-4-8 for ePub

Humans and Technology Press
5325 20th Ave S, Gulfport, FL 33707
v1.1B 250718-1400

Table of Contents

Preliminaries

The series and this book

The Simplifying Series delivers focused starter techniques for selected professions, designed to get you productive fast.

They say that 20% of the technique gets you 80% of the value. So why not learn a good, juicy twenty percent first and get running? Then, level up with other techniques that advance your skill.

My intention is to pick an easy and useful starter kit for various specialties. Project management, software design, product management are entire careers, needing years of study. There is surely a starter kit in each case. That is what I have in mind for this series.

This particular book is for *use cases*. I wrote the full 300-page book "*Writing Effective Use Cases*" (2000). There is nothing wrong with that book, it is still correct and contains details I can't include here. Read it when you want to advance your use case writing. It is missing details on slicing for fine-grained incremental development, so I have a full section on that in this book.

For mapping use cases to user stories and story maps, I wrote the long version in "*Unifying User Stories, Use Cases, Story Maps*" (2024). It describes each technique in depth and shows how to move back and forth between them.

That was still too long. Many people have never seen a use case and don't want to wade through 200 pages of detail. They want to see some examples and get going. That's what this book is for.

Let's go...

Alistair Cockburn
July 21, 2025

Part 1: Just show me a use case

1.1. The use case body parts.

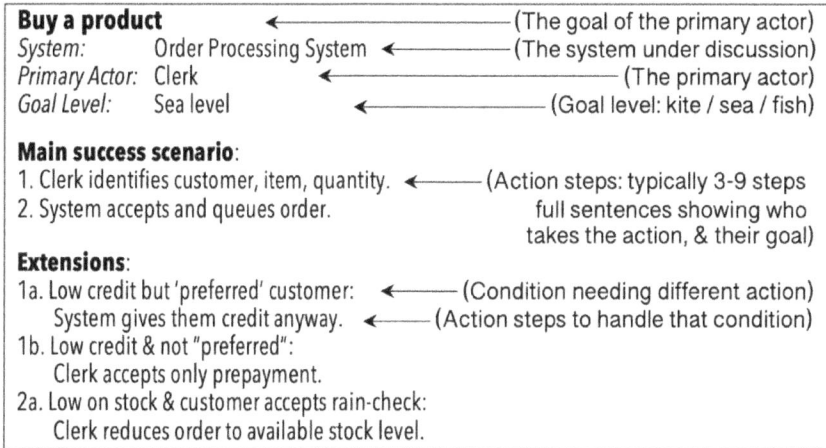

```
Buy a product          ◄──────────────(The goal of the primary actor)
System:      Order Processing System ◄──────(The system under discussion)
Primary Actor:  Clerk              ◄───────────────(The primary actor)
Goal Level:   Sea level           ◄──────────(Goal level: kite / sea / fish)

Main success scenario:
1. Clerk identifies customer, item, quantity. ◄──(Action steps: typically 3-9 steps
2. System accepts and queues order.              full sentences showing who
                                               takes the action, & their goal)
Extensions:
1a. Low credit but 'preferred' customer:  ◄──(Condition needing different action)
    System gives them credit anyway. ◄──(Action steps to handle that condition)
1b. Low credit & not "preferred":
    Clerk accepts only prepayment.
2a. Low on stock & customer accepts rain-check:
    Clerk reduces order to available stock level.
```

Figure 1.1-1. A use case with its parts labeled.

Figure 1.1-1 shows a use case with its parts labeled. This structure applies to all use case styles, casual, formal or other.

1. **The title of the use case** is a verb phrase, the goal to be achieved, present tense, active voice, saying what will be accomplished for the primary actor if and when the use case ends successfully.

2. **The "System"** identifies the outer boundary of what will be considered *outside*, and therefore visible, as opposed to *inside*, and therefore hidden from the reader's view.

3. **The "Primary actor"** is the person, organization, or other system trying to get some goal accomplished. *'Actor'* is a word deliberately chosen so that we don't care whether it is a human, an organization or an automated system.

4. **The "Goal level"** is one of four choices.

"Sea level" indicates a business task of the primary actor, an elementary business process or an atomic database transaction. Typically done in 2-20 minutes, in one sitting.

"Kite level" indicates that the primary actor will need to have multiple interactions with the system over time. It might take days, weeks or years.

"Fish level" indicates that it is a subtask of a sea-level task. It is only ever written because it is too complicated to fit nicely inside its sea-level use case, or else because it is used in multiple use cases.

"Clam level" indicates that this use case should never have been written, it really belongs inside a higher-level use case. While we don't use clam level in use cases themselves, the term is useful to label user stories or work assignments when we split the use case up for development.

Those first four items constitute the header of the use case.

> *Many people omit items 2-4, thinking they are not important. This causes confusion when the number of use cases grows. So be sure to include them.*

5. **The "Main success scenario"** is where you put the steps involved when the goal succeeds in a fairly typical situation. The steps can be numbered or not, and written in flowing paragraphs for easy reading, or on separate lines for better traceability.

6. **The "Action steps"** tell the action. Each step follows a simple grammar: noun, verb, direct object. Each verb is a goal that gets accomplished, so that it can become a use case title in its own right. Typically, 3-9 steps work nicely.

Notice that the action steps do not mention the technology used. Assume you will have both voice and screen interfaces. The words 'identifies,' 'enters, ' 'selects', 'indicates' work well for input; and 'presents' and 'notifies' for output.

7. **The "Extensions" section** is the place to put "but what if" situations that have to be considered. Each entry gives some condition that might be encountered and how it's handled.

8. **An "Extension condition"** is some condition that might be encountered, whether just another way of following a success path, or a possible failure that has to be dealt with.

In the formal style, the number indicates at which step in the main success scenario the condition might be discovered. By convention, the suffix is a letter 'a', 'b', 'c' and so on, indicating different conditions that might be encountered on the same step. There is no ordering implied by the 'a', 'b', or 'c'.

9. **The "Extension handling steps"** are action steps written in the exact same style as the action steps in the main success scenario, in a scenario fragment.

1.2. A dozen use cases to get you started.

Use case 1: Buy a candy

Casual, concrete style:

"Go to the machine and push the button under the Mars bar. It will light up the price on the side. Put in the money. It will release the candy and drop the change. Bring those back.

If it is out of Mars bars, it will say "EMPTY". In that case, choose a Milky Way. If that is also empty, then never mind, don't buy anything, and give me back the money.

If it is out of change, it will say, "EXACT CHANGE ONLY." But that's okay – I want the candy anyway, so, put in the money. It will drop the candy and not give any change. Just bring me the candy."

Formal style:

System:	The candy machine
Primary Actor:	The customer
Goal Level:	Sea level (user task)

Main success scenario:
1. Customer selects candy. Machine shows the price and allows money to be put in.
2. Customer puts in the money.
3. Machine drops the candy and the change.

Extensions:
1a. No more of that candy:
   Machine shows "Empty" and doesn't accept money.

1b. No change available in the machine:
   Machine puts up "Exact change required."

3a. No change available in the machine:
   Machine drops the candy, but not the change.

Use case 2: Buy a product

Casual style:

The Clerk identifies the customer, item, and quantity. The system accepts and queues the order.

If the customer has low credit and is 'preferred', the system gives them credit anyway, otherwise has them pay cash. If stock is low, the system offers them a rain check.

Formal style:

System: Order Processing System
Primary Actor: Clerk
Goal Level: Sea level

Main success scenario:
1. Clerk identifies customer, item, quantity.
2. System accepts and queues order.

Extensions:
1a. Customer has low credit but is "preferred":
        System gives them credit anyway.

1b. Customer has low credit and is not "preferred":
        Clerk accepts only prepayment.

2a. Low on stock & customer accepts rain-check:
        Clerk reduces order to available stock level.

Use case 3: Get cash with "Fast Cash"   *(casual, concrete style)*

Mary, taking her two daughters to the day care center on the way to work, drives up to the ATM, taps her card on the contactless reader, enters her PIN code, and selects FAST CASH (USUAL AMOUNT).

The ATM recalls her usual amount as $35, issues $20 and three $5 bills plus a receipt showing her account balance after the $35 is debited. It resets its screens after each transaction so Mary can drive away and not worry that the next driver will have access to her account.

Mary likes FAST CASH because it avoids the many questions that slow down the interaction. She comes to this particular ATM because it issues $5 bills, which she uses to pay the day care provider, and she doesn't have to get out of her car to use it.

Use case 4: Register for courses   *(formal style)*

System: Course Enrollment System (CES)
Primary Actor: Student
Goal Level: Sea level (user task)

Main success scenario:

1. Student requests to construct a schedule.
2. CES prepares a blank schedule form.
3. CES gets available courses from the Course Catalog System.
4. Student selects up to four primary and two alternate course offerings.
5. For each course, CES verifies that the Student has the necessary prerequisites and adds the Student to the course, marking Student as "enrolled" for that course in the schedule.
6. The Student indicates the schedule is complete, CES saves it.

Extensions:

1a. Student already has a schedule:
    CES brings up the current version of the Student's schedule for editing instead of creating a new one.
1b. Current semester is closed & next semester is not yet open:
    CES lets Student look at courses, but not create a new schedule.
3a. Course Catalog System does not respond:
    CES notifies the Student and the use case ends.
5a. Course full or Student has not fulfilled all prerequisites:
    CES disables selection of that course and notifies the Student.

Use case 5: +Profit from OurApp   *(formal style)*

System: OurApp
Primary Actor: Admin, Vendors, Registered customers
Goal Level: Business summary (kite)

Main success scenario:

1. The admin or the vendor *sets up a new vendor account*.
2. The vendor *adds or edits events, venues, services*, (an admin has to *approve events*), then may *update their account details*.
3. A person *registers themselves* with the app, may *update their account details* or *update their preferences*.
4. A person can *toggle between being a vendor or a customer* for the next period.
5. A registered customer *logs in* with email, Google, Apple ID.
6. A registered customer *locates and registers for an event or service*.
7. A registered customer can *earn tokens*.
8. From a personal menu, a registered customer can *contact support*, *turn notifications on and off*, *change settings*, *see tickets*, and *change preferences*.
9. The admin *collects reports from the app*.
10. The vendor may *cash out payments from users*.

Extensions:

*a. The vendor cancels or doesn't pay: (what happens here?)

(The *underlined phrases* are hyperlinks to sea-level use cases.)

Use case 6: +Manage asset   *(casual, concrete style)*

System:	All systems around asset management
Primary Actor:	All
Goal Level:	Kite level (summary)
Context:	This kite-level use case shows all the movements of a tool from birth to death, serving as the context for the individual sea-level use cases.

Main success scenario:

1. In engineering, *Daniel the designer* creates a new tool's bill of materials in system X, which passes it to system Y, from whence system Z pulls it on a weekly basis.

2. *Susan the sustaining engineer* defines its maintenance schedule in Z, updating the bill of materials as needed.

3. *Mary the manufacturing engineer* approves the birth certificate in Z, which notifies X that the tool is available for use. …

4. *Casey the customer service rep* sees in system Y that the item has been requested and gives it a new destination in system W.

5. *Larry the logistics coordinator* logs its arrival in Z, which notifies *Frank the financial manager* to log the financials. *Tammy the tool technician* tests the tool and loads the results in Z.

6. *Rajesh the resource manager* assigns the tool to <job site>. System V tracks its usage there. When it breaks or reaches its use limit, Rajesh arranges for it to be returned. …

(This continued for three pages. The system names have been cut for confidentiality.)

Use case 7: +Get paid for car accident   *(formal style)*

System:	Insurance company
Primary Actor:	Claimant
Goal Level:	Business summary (kite)

Main success scenario:
1. Claimant submits claim with substantiating data.
2. Insurance company verifies claimant owns a valid policy.
3. Insurance company assigns agent to examine case.
4. Insurance company verifies all details are within policy guidelines.
5. Insurance company pays claimant and closes file.

Extensions:
1a. Submitted data is incomplete:
    .1 Insurance company requests missing information.
    .2. Claimant supplies missing information.
2a. Claimant does not own a valid policy:
    Insurance company denies claim, notifies claimant, records all this, terminates proceedings.
3a. No agents are available at this time.
    (What does the insurance company do here?)
4a. Accident violates basic policy guidelines:
    Insurance company denies claim, notifies claimant, records all this, terminates proceedings.
4b. Accident violates some minor policy guidelines:
    Insurance company begins negotiation with claimant as to amount of payment to be made.

Use case 8: +Handle a Claim   *(formal style)*

System: All systems around claims
Primary Actor: All
Goal Level: Kite level (summary)

Main success scenario:
1. Customer reports a claim to Clerk.
2. Clerk *finds the policy*, ***registers a loss***, and *assigns an adjuster*.
3. Adjuster investigates the claim and *updates the claim*.
4. Adjuster *enters progress notes* over time, *corrects entries* and *sets monies* aside over time.
6. Adjuster receives documentation and *enters bills*.
7. Adjuster *evaluates damages* for claim and *documents the negotiation process* in System.

Extensions:
1a. Submitted data is incomplete:
    1a1. Adjuster requests missing information.
    1a2. Claimant supplies missing information.
        1a2a. Claimant does not reply within time period:
            Adjuster closes claim in System.
2a. Claimant does not own a valid policy:
    2a1. Adjuster *declines claim.*
3a. No agents are available at this time:
    3a1. (What do we do here?)
7a. Claimant notifies adjuster of new claim activity:
    7a1. Clerk reopens claim. Reverts to step 3.

(The *underlined* phrases are hyperlinks to sea-level use cases. "***Register a loss***" is shown on the next page.)

Use case 9: Register a loss   *(formal style)*

System: Claims-handling system
Primary Actor: Clerk
Goal Level: Sea level (user task)
Preconditions: Clerk is already logged in and verified.
                     Clerk has already opened a new loss form

Main success scenario:

Note: To speed up the clerk's work, the System should do its work asynchronously, as soon as the required data is captured. The Clerk can enter data in any order to match the needs of the moment. The following sequence is foreseen as the most likely.

1. Clerk enters insured's policy number or else name and date of incident. System populates available policy information and indicates that claim is matched to policy.
2. Clerk enters basic loss information. System confirms there are no existing, possibly competing claims and assigns a claim number.
3. Clerk enters other loss information specific to claim line.
4. Clerk has System pull other coverage information from other computer systems.
5. Clerk selects and assigns an Adjuster.
6. Clerk confirms they are finished; System saves and triggers acknowledgment to be sent to Agent.

Extensions:

*a. Power failure during loss capture:
   System autosaves intermittently (possibly at certain transaction commit points, open issue).
*b. Claim is not for our company to handle:
   Clerk indicates to System that claim is entered "only for recording purposes" and either continues or ends loss.
1a. Found policy information does not match the insured's information:
   Clerk enters correct policy number or insured name and asks System to populate with new policy index information.

1b. Using search details, System could not find a policy:
Clerk returns to loss and enters available data.

1c. Clerk changed policy number, date of loss, or claim line after initial policy match:
.1. System validates changes, populates loss with correct policy information, validates and indicates that claim is matched to policy.
.a. System cannot validate policy match:
System warns Clerk.
Clerk finds the policy using the search details for "policy."
.2. System warns Clerk to re-evaluate coverage.

1d. Clerk wants to restart a loss which has been interrupted, saved, or needs completion:
Clerk *finds a loss* using search details for "loss." System opens it for editing.

2-5a. Clerk changes claim line previously entered and no line-specific data has been entered:
System presents appropriate line-specific sections of loss based on Clerk entering a different claim line.

2-5b. Clerk changes claim line previously entered and there is data in some of the line-specific fields:
.1. System warns that data exists and asks Clerk to either cancel changes or proceed with new claim line.
.a. Clerk cancels change: System continues with the loss.
.b. Clerk insists on new claim line: System blanks out data which is line specific (it keeps all basic claim-level data).

2c. System detects possible duplicate claim:
.1 System displays a list of possible duplicate claims from within loss database.
.2. Clerk selects and views a claim from the list. (This step may be repeated multiple times.)
.a. Clerk finds that the claim is a duplicate:
Clerk opens duplicate claim for editing if not yet marked completed (based on Clerk's security profile). Clerk may delete any data in previously saved file.

.b. Clerk finds that the claim is not a duplicate:
Clerk returns to loss and completes it.

2d. Preliminary loss information is changed after initial duplicate claim check is done:
System performs duplicate claim check again.

2e. Clerk can have the System save the loss any time before completion of steps 2 through 6.

4-5a. Either claim line or loss description (see business rules) is changed after coverage was reviewed by Clerk:
System warns Clerk to re-evaluate coverage.

6a. Clerk confirms they are finished without completing minimum information:
.1. System warns Clerk it cannot accept the loss without date of loss, insured name or policy number, and handling Adjuster:
.a. Clerk decides to continue entering loss or decides to save without marking complete.
.b. Clerk insists on exiting without entering minimum information:
System discards any intermediate saves and exits.
.2. System warns Clerk it cannot assign claim number without required fields (claim line, date of loss, policy number, or insured name): System directs Clerk to fields that require entry.

6b. Time-out: Clerk has saved the loss temporarily, intending to return; System decides it is time to commit and log the loss, but handling Adjuster has still not been entered:
System assigns default Adjuster (see Business Rules).

That is a use case from a real project, see pages 75-78 of _Writing Effective Use Cases_. Notice in particular extension 6b, which is a quite hidden condition that most techniques won't flush out. I challenge you to write this use case in another format such that everyone involved can review it, and assert it is both complete and correct.

Use case 10: –Log in   *(formal style)*

System: OurApp
Primary Actor: Any user
Goal Level: Fish (subfunction)

Main success scenario:
1. User requests to log in.
2. System offers all the ways of logging in: *Email / password*, *Single Sign On*, *Google*, *Facebook*, *Apple*.
3. The login being successful, the calling use case passes control over to the app as a successful login.

Extensions:
3a. All attempts to log in fail:
      System ends with a note to contact help for further assistance.

(Although it is fish level, Log-in is very complicated. Try your hand at finishing this use case, getting *all* the variations, conditions, failure modes and reset options. For simplicity, write each variant as its own fish level use case. I offer the email/password version next, as a model.)

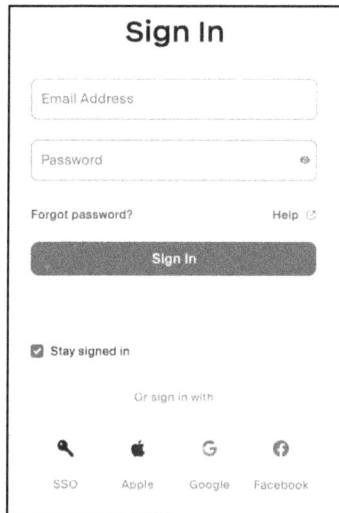

Use case 11: –Log in with email/password *(formal style)*

System:	OurApp
Primary Actor:	Any user
Goal Level:	Fish (subfunction)
Trigger:	User asked to log in using email plus password.

Main success scenario:
1. System collects email and password from user.
2. System validates email and password are correct.
3. System marks login as successful.

Extensions:
1a. System sees that the account has been locked from previous
    unsuccessful login attempts:
    .1. System asks user to *reset password*. or contact customer service.
2a. The email/password combination is not correct:
    System gives the user two more tries to get them right.
2b. All tries have been used and still not correct:
    .1. System marks the account as locked.
    .2. System notifies the user the account is being locked and to
        contact customer service.
    .3. System ends this use case with login marked unsuccessful.
2c. At any time, the user can ask to reset their password:
    System lets user *reset password*.

Use case 12: –Save report   *(formal style)*

System:	OurApp
Primary Actor:	Any user
Goal Level:	Fish (subfunction)

Main success scenario:

1. System sees that report's status is "named" and "modified."
2. System updates the data in the Report List, saves the report specs in the file system.
3. System changes the report's status to "unmodified."

Extensions:

1a. User asked for "Save as…" instead of "Save":

System behaves the same as the report being "unnamed."

1b. The report status is "unnamed":

.1. System prompts the user for the new report name.

.2. User enters name.

.a. System sees that no other report already has that name:

System adds the report to the Report List, saves the report specs in that file, sets the report's status to "named" and "unmodified".

.b. System sees that another report already has that name:

.1. System asks permission to overwrite the other report.

.a. User accepts:

System saves report specs in the existing file, updates the data in the Report List entry, changes status to "named" "unmodified."

.b. User declines:

System aborts the Save operation.

1.3. Notes on these use cases.

We haven't dug into use cases in detail yet, but it is still worthwhile to look at some notes on these examples.

Use case 1: Buy a Candy

The top part is written in *casual* style, ordinary sentences in paragraph form. It is *concrete*, meaning that instead of saying "user" or "amount," it gives a concrete example. People find these easy to read, and they are also good at generalizing from concrete examples.

This one is written as if describing to someone over the phone what to do. Use cases are so easy to understand because they mirror perfectly how we *speak* a process, describing the entire main success case before explaining what to do in each alternative situation.

The second part is written in the formal style, with header, line numbers and a separate extensions section. The first thing I wish to show by having the same use case in both styles is that both styles are fine, use whichever suits your situation best.

The casual style is faster to write and easier to read, but usually is incomplete. It is a good way to sketch what you want. Write the formal style when you want to be really clear and to have a good structure for double checking that nothing was forgotten.

Use case 2: Buy a Product

This, from a real project, is also shown in both styles so you can see them side by side. Sharp readers may notice one corner case still not mentioned. It's easiest to see in the formal style, which is why I tend to use that more often.

Use case 3: Get cash with "Fast Cash"

This particular casual, concrete story was written in the mid-1990s by a usability expert at Hewlett-Packard in one of my classes. Notice how she included certain emotional motivations that make it a bit more interesting to read, and also help the designers get into the mind of the user, to understand *why* certain features are included.

Use case 4: Register for courses

A larger use case, taken from the book *Patterns for Effective Use Cases* by Steve Adolph and Paul Bramble.

Take special note of step 4. I highlight this step to show that you don't need to get tangled up in weird numbering rules, but rather, write directly to another human. Your writing can be both specific and readable at the same time.

Never mention the technology for input and output. I write assuming that the user interface will be both voice- and screen-based. This makes the use cases more stable over time and also more readable.

Use case 5: +Profit from OurApp

This kite-level use case details *everything* that was offered by this app. I wrote this with the founder after she got burned by her contract programmers. She had used an agile approach with just user stories, and they kept leaving out things that she needed but were not listed in the user stories. We found all the places where she had had contractual difficulties just by looking for the alternative situations in this one use case.

Prefixing the title with a '+' is a useful trick to show the reader that it is kite level even before they open it. The '+' stores nicely in file names and sorts so that kite-level use cases are separated from the sea-level use cases. It provides a handy visual tip to the reader looking at a long list of use case names.

Use case 6: +Manage asset

This *kite-level* use case describes the entire lifecycle of a piece of equipment, from birth to death. It took several pages to cover that entire lifecycle, even writing in a fairly condensed form.

I wrote it in concrete, casual style because it was going to be read by people at all levels of the company with no training in use cases. I needed them to understand—and if need be, argue with—the contents of the use case without any prior warning about the form or format being used. Hence, I used the name alliteration, and anything else I could think of to make it easy to read.

Use case 7: +Get paid for car accident

This high-level use case is a kite-level use case showing overall business flow. It got expanded into use cases 8 and 9, which follow.

If you read carefully, you will see the driving difference between this and the next one is the *System* being discussed.

- In this use case the *System* is the entire company. This use case's purpose was to provide context of the overall process, not to name and link lower-level use cases.
- In the following one, "+Handle a claim," which was part of a requirements package, the *System* is "All the systems around claims." You can see it is more detailed, specifically naming and linking sub-use cases.

I hope you see how important it is to make clear what *System* is being discussed. Leaving that off causes much confusion.

Notice also the question in one of the extensions. This is a good way to mark places that need research. Books usually only show fully completed use cases, which robs you of a chance to see how they appear in flight. I fill my intermediate work with all sorts of questions and loud notes, so everyone can see what's decided and what's not.

Use case 8: +Handle a claim

This was the kite-level use case linking a number of sea-level ones. The *System* included multiple subsystems, which got named in the sea-level use cases (for example, use case 9, "Register a loss").

A kite-level use case like this serves as documentation of a macro process and also as a table of contents into the other use cases.

Use case 9: Register a loss

This is the use case used by Fireman's Fund Insurance Company in spec'ing their new claims system around 1999 (It is included with other examples from that project in *"Writing Effective Use Cases."*)

All claims pass through this use case. I was delighted to get permission to include it. The manager said, "There's nothing confidential or secret about this process. All insurance companies have to do the same thing; it's governed by law."

It took several weeks to write, not because of typing, but because every circumstance had to be investigated. Extension 6b, for example, caught me off guard. When would you have discovered this?

Finally, notice that there are only six steps in the main success scenario. The action happens in all the things that can vary along the way, pages of them. Having a short main scenario and a long list of extensions is quite common in such a main use case.

Use case 10: –Log in

Logging in doesn't provide business value to the user, but the flow is complex, so it gets its own use case. It's fish level.

Notice that I also broke out the even lower-level use cases for email/password, single sign-on, Google, etc. I started writing them all in one use case, but as it became unreadable, I decided to break them all out into their separate spaces.

As with the '+' prefix, the '–' prefix indexes nicely in the file system to separate fish-level from sea-level use cases.

Use case 11: –Log in with email/password

Notice the *Trigger* in the header. I use that rarely, but here we want the writing to start after the use case has already been triggered. Capturing the *Trigger* is particularly useful for time-based triggers, such as "Every morning at 7:00 a.m."

Use case 12: –Save report

This fish-level use case describes a function that is too complicated to embed in another use case, but doesn't serve a complete business transaction. Other typical similar ones are *Pay for shopping cart, Log in,* and the *Find a <whatever>* search function.

Part 2: What, exactly, is a use case?

*A use case is all the ways of using a system
to achieve a goal of a particular user.*

—Ivar Jacobson

Ivar Jacobson invented use cases in the late 1980s. I learned them from him in 1992, used them, deconstructed, tagged and labeled all the parts, and wrote *Writing Effective Use Cases* in 2000. That book has become the standard reference for use cases.

Although Ivar and I were always in agreement in our interpretations, we sometimes used slightly different words. In 2024, we sat together and wrote a short foundation document showing our agreement. See [https://alistaircockburn.com/Articles/Use-Case-Foundation-Ivar-Alistair]. Everything I write in here (and in my other writings and presentations) is compatible with that foundation document.

Here are the key points in this chapter:

1. Their greatest value is keeping the entire organization aligned as to what system is being developed. Serving as a scaffold for research and as a detailed spec are wonderful but still secondary benefits.

2. A use case can be thought of as any of:
    - a behavioral specification for a system,
    - a way to describe a process,
    - a generic writing format capturing branching behaviors.

3. A use case specifies the actions of the system on all sides. It does not specify data in detail or user interface at all.

4. Use cases nest, because both the title and the steps name goals.

5. Yes, you can write and develop use cases incrementally.

2.1. What *is* a use case?

Ivar Jacobson is very clear about the definition:

> *A use case is all the ways of using a system*
> *to achieve a goal of a particular user.*

A use case shows the various ways a user might succeed or fail to accomplish some goal. It is a *collector of scenarios* held together by a *common user goal*. That goal, which becomes the name of the use case, is shown to succeed in some scenarios and shown to fail in other scenarios. The use case collects all those scenarios together, listed under that goal. That's what a use case is, and its structure.

If you squint a bit, though, you can see three different ways to think about and make good use of them:

View 1. A use case specifies the behavior of a system.

Use cases are most commonly used to capture the behavioral requirements for software systems.

They show the behavior of the system as it interacts with the actors in its environment. They don't show the data details, the interface protocols, timing, security, or many other things needed to design the system. They show only the interactions between the system and these external actors.

Thus, we say that a use case specifies ***all, but <u>only</u>*** the ***<u>behavioral</u>*** requirements for a system.

It shows *all* the behaviors, because it catches *all* the variations and corner cases. It shows *only* behaviors because it does not detail the data, performance, or other requirements.

It's really good at what it does, and it doesn't do the other things. Pick it up when you need it, and put it down when you don't.

View 2. A use case describes a process.

A little more generally, we don't have to use this tool only for *software* systems nor only for requirements specification, but rather, we can use it to describe any sort of process. In fact, Ivar and his team used it in the 1990s mainly for business process modeling assignments.

Use cases are equivalent to many other process description formats. You might use flow charts, UML activity diagrams, or other process diagramming tools. It is, however, the only *textual* process description notation I know of. All the others are graphical formats.

If you want a highly readable textual description of a process, use cases are your game, and they are very good at that.

3. A use case is just a writing format that captures branching behaviors nicely.

Information has shape. Different kinds of information fit naturally into different containers:

- A task list fits into a simple list.
- When the information has a flow and a certain amount of branchiness, it fits neatly into a use case.
- Once the branching becomes too complicated, you need something like a table or a finite state machine. Tables are great when you need to check that every combination of factors has been considered and documented.
- Mind maps, book outlines, data structures and formulas all have their own natural shapes. A drawing is perfect for describing user interfaces.

If you have steps with branches (but not too many), then it matches what a use case naturally supports. A friend of mine used use cases to write contracts for his subcontractors. He found that the extensions section captured nicely the situations he needed to protect. Perfect.

When the information doesn't have that shape, use something else. Don't stick with the use case shape when you need to capture something else. Embed a table, formula, screenshot, or state machine directly into your use case if you need.

Here's what happens when you put a data structure into a use case:

The client showed me a 30-page use case. It was well written and readable, but boring. It said: The system asks this, the user provides that, the system asks this other, the user provides that other, and so on.

I said, "It looks like the user is filling in a form or something."

The client picked up a stack of forms with a red rubber spine and said, "Yes, the 10-955 form we need them to enter here."

I said, "How about you just write one sentence: 'The user enters the information from the 10-955.'" Print that page and staple the form to that sheet?"

Old school – but I'm glad to say he did exactly that.

The point is that a printed form already has a shape that suits its purpose, and that shape is not what use cases are so good at.

Someone else sent me this question:

I have this use case in which the clerk is asked to change something about the insurance policy during its term. Depending on what they ask to change, it changes either just the price or it changes quite a lot.

Originally, I put each type of change into its own use case, but it seemed to fit the user's goal and was more meaningful to the business users to have it as just one use case.

Each type of change may or may not cause the premium to change. An increase in cover will result in additional premium, which could be collected in a number of ways (dd, credit card, cheque). Reduction in cover may result in a pro rata refund if the cover has been paid for in full upfront, but not if it's a monthly policy.

How I should deal with all these scenarios?

A table is called for here. Initially, I started by matching his text:

Use case: Change policy mid-term
1. Customer requests a change to their policy.
2. Clerk selects which actions to take and the cost/policy changes according to the following table:

Requested change	Change to policy	Change to premium	Mode of payment/ refund

But then I saw that "Mode of payment/refund" is generic – it shouldn't be elaborated in this use case at all. Hence:

Use case: Change policy mid-term
1. Customer requests a change to their policy.
2. Clerk selects which actions to take and the cost/policy changes according to the following table:

Requested change	Change to policy	Change to premium	Amount to be paid / refunded

3. Clerk "*collects payment from or refunds to customer.*"

Notice the shape of your information. Your communication will be light and clear when you use a container that matches that shape. Feel free to mix them together for the best effect.

In the end, you can write use cases to

- specify a software system,
- describe a process, or
- document whatever needs its special shape.

Since this is a short book, I will just talk about specifying the behavior of software systems. Experiment with the other uses.

2.2. Use cases align an organization.

The highest value use cases provide is not the specification itself, but the way it keeps an organization aligned on what is being delivered.

Everyone in the organization reads at least the top-level use cases. That includes the sponsoring executives, business managers, business analysts, tech leads, individual programmers, testers, delivery people, and trainers. Each one needs to know what to sell, what to build, what to test, what to train on. If they have different views of what will get built, that mistake is more expensive than anything else.

This means the use cases must be easy to read.

If you write beautifully structured and tight but long, complicated specifications with every detail included, then those people won't read them. That results in conflict and wasted energy. Strangely, the more detail you put into the use cases, the lower their total value.

A client executive taught me that I was missing this very point and told me I should highlight it (which I'm doing here).

Another client said their very small set of very simple use cases saved the project. When he sent me the use cases, I found them so simple as to be embarrassing. I asked him how such simple use cases could "save his project." He replied:

> "With the other ways we have written our requirements, our programmers don't really understand them. They get distracted by 'shiny objects' and program a bunch of things our clients don't want. Then, after taking too long, what they deliver doesn't match what the clients requested.

> "With these use cases, everyone understood what was supposed to be delivered. The programmers stayed on track and delivered what the clients wanted.

> They saved our project."

You can see that the value of the use cases is not related to how long or complicated they are.

At another client:

> *At the end of the training workshop, the field operatives wrote on a flipchart just the seven sentences of the main success scenario of their main use case.*
>
> *The project manager looked at that flipchart and said, "There is not a single sentence on there that is within the scope of the project."*
>
> *Silence ensued, as you might imagine.*

Although embarrassing, at least they found the misalignment after writing just the first part of the first use case. "I guess it's good to find out now!" one sponsor said.

Keep the writing simple and readable. You can afford to capture the details in side documents, preserving the readability of the use cases.

Reiterating, the **first value** of use cases is keeping an organization aligned on what's being built.

The **second value** is that use cases provide a scaffold for business analysts to think up and investigate difficult corner cases before the developers and testers do. It is the only technique I know of that provides this.

The **third value** is providing a detailed specification to the developers and the testers, showing the context of each scenario and how each alternative condition should unfold.

The **fourth** and final value of the use cases is that the list of use case names provides a great organizing structure for project management. The use case names serve as an index into everything that needs to get built. You can associate schedule, cost, risk, team assignments, etc., with the use case names. This is independent of the content of the use cases, using just the use case names themselves.

2.3. A use case specs the actions of the system on all sides. It does not spec data or user interface.

A use case is a *specification*. When done, your set of use cases should show <u>all</u> the actions an application or system will have to take under <u>all</u> circumstances.

In order to accomplish this, each use case has to explicitly name every condition it will encounter and how to handle each. It will also name every back-end system it will have to interact with.

To make all this work, we need two new terms:

Primary actor: Something with its own behavior (hardware, software, person or organization) that will kick the application into action, requesting some service from it. The primary actors are the ones with the goals that become use case names.

Secondary actor: Something (hardware, software, person or organization) that our system will trigger into action, whether just to notify it or to get information back.

The only real difference between primary and secondary actors is who initiates the conversation. The primary actors trigger our use cases, the secondary actors are called out in the action steps *inside* the use cases.

It is important to name *all* secondary actors and what services they provide. It makes a big difference whether designing a service is part of *this* project or there is already a service that should be used.

For example, if it is within this project's assignment to design and program the user authentication, there will be a step:

System <u>*authenticates user*</u>.

"<u>*Authenticates user*</u>" is underlined and hyperlinked to its elaboration because it is too complicated to embed in the use case that uses it. It is a separate (fish-level) use case.

However, if there already is an authentication service that should be used, that service is a secondary actor, and the step will read:

> System has the authentication service authenticate the user.

Notice how this sentence

- makes clear that this service already exists and should not be developed by the programmers on this project,
- identifies an external interface that has to be researched, and
- does *not* call out a lower-level use case that will be expanded. This sentence is all that needs to be said.

Since use cases name those back-end systems, it is important to include tech team members as well as business users in the writing of the use cases. Neither group can get them all correct on their own.

Use cases capture all the behaviors and interactions of the system, but not the data details. Well, they do identify the data, but only briefly, at low precision. Here are two examples:

> User provides their personal information.
> User provides name, address, phone number, etc.

Read more about this in **Core Concept #1:** *Manage Precision.*

You will, of course, have to write the data descriptions and all those other details—security, performance, UI, etc.—eventually. Put them into side documents, so as not to lose the easy readability of the use case itself. See **Core Concept #6:** *Write just the needs, not the encyclopedia,* and **Core Concept #7:** *Sacrifice perfection for readability.*

A common mistake is to write the use cases really well and then forget to capture all the other requirements. Don't do that.

In the end, make sure every user and system action is accounted for, make sure the use cases are easy to read, briefly identify the data that passes back and forth. Append data details, security, safety, and performance requirements at the end or in side documents.

2.4. Use cases nest, because both the title and the steps name goals.

We achieve a goal by breaking it into subgoals, and those into further subgoals as needed. This is fairly normal, we do this all the time.

The title of the use case names a goal. We write each step in the use cases as a subgoal needed to achieve the top-level goal. It won't surprise you that we can break the subgoals down into further subgoals that have to be achieved. This means that any verb phrase in any step can be the name of another, lower-level use case!

Most of the time, we don't need to break out a step into another use case, because most of the time the step is sufficiently clear and straightforward, we know what it means.

> "Clerk marks the order as ready for shipment."

This is simple, we don't need to expand *how* that gets done. That is for the user interface designers to design.

Kite-level use cases, on the other hand, are intended to be broken down. Each individual step in a kite-level use case is likely to be a sea-level use case, which will have its own elaboration.

Here is a kite level use case to illustrate:

> The supervisor *logs in* each morning and *sets up the application for the day*, then logs out and passes the device to the daily worker.
> 1. The daily worker *logs in.*
> 2. Every time a certain event happens, the daily worker *records the details of the event*

The purpose of this use case is to show the entire business process of a day in the life of the application. *Log in* is a fish-level use case. *Set up the application for the day* and *Record the details of the event* are sea-level.

Occasionally, a subgoal inside a sea-level use case is complicated, having its own failure conditions and alternative success paths. If you find everything becomes easier to understand if it has its own space, then create a fish-level use case elaborating that subgoal.

Log in (*Authenticate user*) is such a one, because people can get authenticated in so many ways, and there are many ways to recover from mistakes.

Another one will be this:

> "Customer *pays for items in cart and arranges shipping*."

It would be inappropriate to elaborate all the details around paying for the items in a cart inside the use case that covers searching for items, gathering them in the cart and finally paying for them. Doing so would make the use case long and hard to follow (see **Core Concept #2:** *Understand that verbs imply duration*). So we put this fish-level use case into its own space.

Just don't get too carried away with sub-sub-use cases. Having lots of tiny use cases makes the overall system harder to understand.

The nesting of use cases creates a sort of sailboat view of all the use cases for a system:

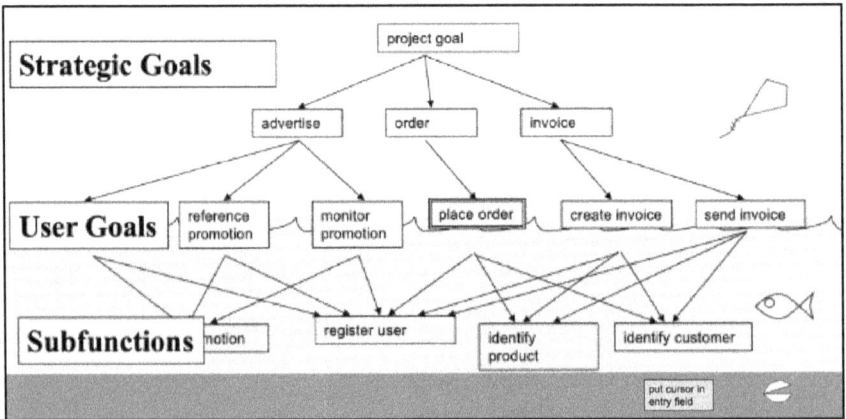

Figure 2.4-1. The "sailboat" view of how use cases connect.

Here, we see a single use case at the top, whose sole purpose is to connect the kite-level use cases. Those kite-level use cases break into any number of sea-level use cases. Fish-level use cases only get written when they are used in multiple places or are too complicated to include inside the higher-level use case. 'Clam' was a tag coined to indicate it is too low level to be given its own use case.

On my first project using use cases, we had about 240 use cases, whose top-level one was really just a starting point to hold the graph together. Then there were perhaps half a dozen kite-level use cases, around 180 sea-level use cases, and 30 fish-level.

On this fixed-price project, we walked the entire graph as the basis for the contract, starting at the very top and going down through all of them, asking two questions to each of the business and the development contractors:

Business: "Is this what you want? and will you know if it's there when you get it?"

Development: "Do you understand this? and can you build it?"

And at the very end: "And is that everything?"

From those, the contract was signed. A year and a half later, they were examined for final delivery. In short, they worked.

Read more in **Core Concept #3:** *Decompose verbs into shorter-duration verbs.*

Part 3: Write, develop & deliver incrementally

A totally finished set of use cases captures all scenarios with all extension handling. However, you don't have to write, develop, or deliver them all at once. In fact, that is probably not a good strategy, for several reasons.

Writing all the use cases up front, developing them all in one block, and delivering the system all in one delivery is sub-optimal because

- what you thought at the beginning will be needed is not what your users will find they need when they start using it,
- you won't know what you have wrong until your users start using it, and
- you will delay the first development and delivery as you spend time investigating and writing all the use cases fully.

This has been the experience of projects since before I even started researching the question in 1991. It has gotten only worse, not better, as both systems and users have advanced.

This is where "writing a use case" meets "project management." It is not about what a use case looks like when it's done, but how it evolves along with your conversations with the users, the developers and the finances.

For that reason, I include here a small preamble on *early learning*, which underlies everything else in this chapter. Let's look at *why* we want to do this, then a simple motivating example to get started, and then some detailed techniques and strategies.

3.1. Preamble: *Early learning* for the win.

Early learning is the advanced form of risk reduction. In ordinary risk reduction, you ask: "Will we get there, going as we are going?", "Do we have adequate people on the team?", "Will we hit time and budget targets?" and "Will people use this?"

Early learning sets up better questions: "How can we help our team work *better* together?", "What would the users use *even more* than what we originally planned?" and "Where are the difficult places and what can we do about them?" These questions have been the holy grail for as long as I've been around.

Fine-grained incremental development with user viewings and staged deployment are the best way we know to answer these questions. That is why I am writing about incremental development in detail, and include *Walking Skeleton* as the bonus tip in **Core Concepts.**

The thing is that you are making *decisions in advance* about how your users will use the system. A certain percentage of your decisions will be right (yayyy!), and a certain percentage wrong (ow!). The more decisions you pour into your requirements at the beginning, the more mistakes you will bake into the final system.

You will research the mistaken ideas, the programmers will program them, you will deploy them to users who will not use them or will immediately ask for something different. Each mistaken request in the use cases is expensive in terms of development effort.

Worse, as you spend time writing *everything* before starting, you delay that first delivery that provides value, payment and information. This is the "time cost of delay," the financial impact of delaying delivery past the minimum.

The art is to decide which use cases to elaborate, to what level of detail, and then how to slice for development and deployment.

There are two hazards here: One is that you take all the time you need to nail everything down before programming starts. That costs you not only the "time cost of delay," but also time and money when you find a feature was wrong in the first place: You throw that part away and redo the use case, programming and testing for the new idea. "Time cost of delay" plus "cost of rework" is bad news.

The opposite hazard is full "agile" development, never writing an extension until it's time to program it. The trouble is that some business rules require alignment across departments. It can take weeks to get agreement on some of them. If you assume all business rules can be written on the fly, researching none of them in advance, you will delay the project because you didn't start investigating those ones ahead of time.

To steer between these two errors requires that you scan ahead all the time: Look for "difficult" extensions that you have to start discussion on well in advance, as opposed to "easy" ones, which you can defer until needed. This steering requires not only good eyes, but constant discussion between the business experts and the programmers.

To help you steer and scan ahead, sketch the main use cases to start with. Look for both high-value and high-risk areas. With an overall direction in hand, dig into the details in a just-in-time manner. Develop and deliver the fewest features to start with; add onto them as you and your users get experience with the system.

Create a *Walking Skeleton* of everything: of the use case set, of the user process, of a single use case, of a complicated business rule, of the technical architecture. Those help you decide when to add more breadth to your system, and when you can go deeper into a feature.

What this chapter describes is a way of optimizing timing and energy to get the most effective end results. It saves the project time, money and energy.

Of course, if you are writing use cases for a fixed-price, fixed-scope contract, you have limited ability to play this game – you will need to write them all up front. To the extent your client allows you to play the incremental development game, the better off your results will be. Your mileage may vary, as they say.

3.2. Slicing a simple example: Buy a candy.

Use Case 1b: Buy a candy
> *System:*   The candy machine
> *Primary Actor:* The customer
> *Goal Level:*   Sea level

Main success scenario:
1. Customer selects candy; machine shows the price and allows money to be put in.
2. Customer puts in the money.
3. Machine drops the candy and the change.

Extensions:
1a. No more of that candy:
>   Machine shows "Empty" and doesn't accept money.
1b. No change available in the machine:
>   Machine puts up "Exact change required."
3a. No change available in the machine:
>   Machine drops the candy but no change.

We start by asking ourselves, what is the *least* we can develop that will produce a functioning machine? We are looking for something that might be too simple to put into use, but which still connects the parts of the machine to show the baby system working. This is called a *Walking Skeleton*. You'll be astonished at how often you can actually use a *Walking Skeleton* of the system.

For a *Walking Skeleton* of the candy machine, we need:

1. Some way to select a candy. We can get away with just one candy. "Selecting" is nothing more than pushing a button.
2. The candy is free. We can add pricing and coin handling later.
3. The machine drops the candy on the button push.

That's our *Walking Skeleton*, just enough to wire the main parts of the system together and have it do something. It's the first of what I'll call "slices" for development. This first slice tests the development process and gives us a functioning though non-commercial machine.

For slice 2, we add some simple coin handling:

1. The machine accepts and counts the money put in, but doesn't give change. This gets us the calculating of coins and prices.
2. The candy only gets dropped when there is sufficient money.
3. If there is a coin slot that needs to be opened, this also forces testing that the coin slot opens when the selection is made and closes when the candy is dropped.

For slice 3, we might add more products and buttons, still all at the same price, still needing exact change. This might actually be a machine we can deliver and put into use.

For slice 4, we add different prices, and so on, until we have the entire use case.

Here is the fraction of the use case implemented in the first delivery:

Use Case 1, delivery 1: Buy candy, one price, exact change only
Main success scenario:
1. Customer selects candy *(only one possible)*; machine shows the price (*only one price supported*) and allows money to be put in.
2. Customer puts in the money.
3. Machine drops the candy ~~and the change~~ when the price of the candy is reached.
Extensions:
~~1a. No more of that candy:~~
~~Machine shows "Empty" and doesn't accept money.~~
1b. No change available in the machine:
Machine puts up "Exact change required."
3a. No change available in the machine:
Machine drops the candy, but no change.

Working in this way is fabulously effective, and practiced by the most advanced companies. I offer you the following true story, told to me by a person in one of my classes.

A large, international merchandise chain decided to put RFID tags in all their products.

RFID, or Radio Frequency Identification tags, are the little tags they use to track inventory movements, and also to catch you if you walk out of the store without paying.

They would have their suppliers buy the RFID tags from them to put them into the products. The system to be built was to let all the different suppliers order RFID tags for all the products they carried. This was going to be a fairly large project.

The development team asked who their biggest supplier was, and what item they supplied the most of.

Their first delivery was a screen with just <u>one</u> button, to order 1,000 RFID tags of that exact item from that supplier. If the supplier needed 8,000 tags, they pushed the button eight times.

They developed and deployed that system to the supplier in ONE WEEK!

After that, they asked what that same supplier's second most ordered item was, and added a second button.

Then they repeated that scenario with a second supplier.

At this point, they had a working and delivered system that supported multiple suppliers and multiple items. From there, they expanded their system to all the suppliers and inventory items.

(After he told me this story, I asked him, "What the heck are you doing in my class???")

Please use that story as inspiration to deliver less, sooner, while still delivering value.

3.2. Sketch-and-expand, the writing strategy.

Before describing the sketch-and-expand strategy, I'll tell the story of a fixed-price project where we had to write all the use cases in advance.

My first-ever project based on use cases was Project "Winifred," a fixed-price, fixed-scope project described in detail in Surviving Object-Oriented Projects *(1997).*

We spent several weeks writing 240 use cases in casual style, then more weeks listing the external interfaces and other requirements. We used all of that to estimate UI complexity, database complexity, the other interfaces that would need to be developed, and whatever else was needed to construct a project plan and bid. The whole process took several months. It was painful but necessary for the bid.

The use cases formed the basis for the project. For contract acceptance at the start, we spent two days walking through all the use cases in detail with the IT director and the business analysts. A year-and-a-half later, the same use cases were used to evaluate the completion of the project.

In other words, the use cases worked as intended.

In truth, we didn't find or cover every failure condition. This is common with casual use cases: They are not generally intended to be 100% complete. And yes, that did cost us when we hit one of those undetected failure conditions.

However, there was goodwill and good communication between all the parties. The project delivered on time and not too badly over cost. It was generally considered a successful project.

Most of you will not be writing use cases for a fixed-price contract, so you don't need to write them all in advance. You are either writing for something being developed internally, or you have a good relationship with the developers and can work incrementally.

In those situations, the following is a good way to work. It allows you to steer your writing energy to fit the risk.

Step 1. Write down in half a page or less the purpose of the system, who it should please, its reason for existing.

This is your touchpoint for everything that follows. It keeps you centered. Yes, of course you can change it. At half a page, it is the shortest description of your system and the easiest to update.

Step 2. List all the primary and secondary actors that will interact with your system.

This list is not likely to change much. Together with your short statement of purpose, this helps you direct your energies.

Step 3. Brainstorm and list the main sea-level goals your primary actors will have.

This is your starter *"Actor-Goal"* list. It lives very well in a spreadsheet, or even better, a spreadsheet-like database (I like Airtable for this, it's almost perfect for use cases).

Stare at your Actor-Goal list carefully. This is the list of services your system will offer the outside world. Trim it to the few most important, most critical ones to develop and deploy.

Have the lead developers also work on this list. Have them include those that they sense will give them development trouble. You may want to develop a bit of those ones early, just to manage the development risk.

Story: At one company, the boss asked the lead business analyst to sketch the possible things they could work on. She listed almost a page of kite-level use case names.

They sat together and selected half a dozen to expand. She then listed the main use cases for those, ending with a list over a page long. They subset and expanded like this until they settled on the most important system and use cases to develop next.

Step 4. Write a kite-level use case that covers all those early and critical sea-level use cases. One or two, you shouldn't need more.

Hunt for failure and extension conditions to your kite-level use case. Those will indicate something about the complexity in your system that you otherwise might not think about yet.

Refer to the use case examples given in Chapter 1, particularly the kite-level use cases #5 and #8.

Step 5. Choose some sea-level use cases to investigate closely. Expand them one at a time in this way:

1. Write the main success scenario carefully.
2. Brainstorm and list *all* the conditions that could cause *any* different behavior.

List the conditions, but *don't* dig into their handling just yet. Listing the conditions is easy, fun, and well worth the energy at this point. Working out the handling is hard, tiring, and best left for later, in a just-in-time manner.

Step 6. Review your work with business and tech experts. Select the extensions to expand in detail, the use cases scenarios and extensions to develop for early value and early risk mitigation.

Step 7. From here on, you are in a game of repeating step 6 forever:

1. Add scenarios to add value.
2. Expand extensions to discover complicated or hidden rules.
3. Do these in time to have them ready for the programmers.

This is a game of peeking ahead at what you *might* need, detailing things you think will cause trouble or deliver value. You are balancing three things:

- Careful exploration of the business value. Tune what you write, develop, and deploy to what will be used and valued.
- Careful exploration of risk and complexity. Keep looking ahead at failure conditions, because those often cost disproportionate amounts of work to handle.

- Careful control of the energy expended in writing. It costs a lot of energy to write a request for software, whether you are writing use cases or any other form.

In the end, you will have to describe, the developers will have to program, and the testers will have to test every possible situation. You just don't need to do it all at once.

3.2. Slicing development, in detail.

Incremental development has been a best practice since at least the 1960s. However, most people look at a use case and think that they have to develop and build it all in one go. This works for small and simple use cases, but not for larger ones.

This chapter is a short tutorial on how to approach use cases with an eye to fine-grained incremental development. Developing this way allows you to show progress to the project stakeholders, reduces development risk, and allows you to deliver something valuable early.

The simplest way to slice a use case for incremental development is to cut every sentence out and hand it to the appropriate developer as a development assignment. It sort of works... sort of. I met a business analyst who did exactly that when working with an offshore team one time, so it's not impossible. But we can do better.

In what follows, I present six ideas you can try. Use Case 4, *Register for Courses*, illustrates them nicely. I'll merge the first two sentences of the use case to make it easier to follow.

To make it easier to follow the development sequence, I copy the use case out each time to show each increment of the growing system, with the new part in *underlined italics*.

Here are the six ideas:

Idea #1. The first and last lines of the main success scenario often make a *Walking Skeleton* of the business process and a great first development slice.

Main success scenario:
1. Student requests to construct a schedule. CES prepares a blank schedule form.
2. CES gets available courses from the Course Catalog System.
3. Student selects up to four primary and two alternate course offerings.
4. For each course, CES verifies that the Student has the necessary prerequisites and adds the Student to the course, marking the Student as "enrolled" for that course in the schedule.
5. The Student indicates the schedule is complete. CES saves it.

If we pick out the first and the last steps, we get:

Main success scenario:
1. Student requests to construct a schedule. CES prepares a blank schedule form.
5. The Student indicates the schedule is complete. CES saves it.

That is the *Walking Skeleton* of the use case: the system constructs an empty schedule and saves it. It makes a great first slice.

Notice how we did this with the candy machine:

Main success scenario:
1. Customer selects candy.
3. Machine drops the candy and the change.

Look for this pattern in your use cases. See if you can find *Walking Skeletons* for the example use cases in Chapter 1.

Idea 2: Each sentence in the main success scenario and each simple extension gets its own development slice.

Let's continue with that same use case. It is a hefty one and benefits from being sliced and programmed, even deployed, in stages.

Slice 1: The Walking Skeleton (as we have seen)

> 1. Student requests to construct a schedule. CES prepares a blank schedule form.
> 5. The Student indicates the schedule is complete. CES saves it.

Slice 2: But the Student already has a schedule

> 1. Student requests to construct a schedule. CES prepares a blank schedule form.
> 5. The Student indicates the schedule is complete. CES saves it.
> **Extensions:**
> *1a. Student already has a schedule: CES brings up the current version of the Student's schedule for editing instead of creating a new one.*

Slice 3: Connect to the Course Catalog System (this one for risk reduction)

> 1. Student requests to construct a schedule. CES prepares a blank schedule form.
> *2. CES gets available courses from the Course Catalog System.*
> 5. The Student indicates the schedule is complete. CES saves it.
> **Extensions:**
> 1a. Student already has a schedule: CES brings up the current version of the Student's schedule for editing instead of creating a new one.

Slice 4: Course Catalog System doesn't respond

> 1. Student requests to construct a schedule. CES prepares a blank schedule form.
> 2. CES gets available courses from the Course Catalog System.
> 5. The Student indicates the schedule is complete. CES saves it.
> **Extensions:**
> 1a. Student already has a schedule: CES brings up the current version of the Student's schedule for editing instead of creating a new one.
> *2a. Course Catalog System does not respond:*
> *CES notifies the Student and the use case ends.*

To implement step 3, we'll want several slices. This is explained in detail in **Idea 3**, "Implement just part of a step as its own slice".

Slices 5, 6 & 7: Student selects courses

> 1. Student requests to construct a schedule. CES prepares a blank schedule form.
> 2. CES gets available courses from the Course Catalog System.
> *3. Student selects up to four primary and two alternate course offerings.*
> 5. The Student indicates the schedule is complete. CES saves it.
> **Extensions:**
> 1a. Student already has a schedule: CES brings up the current version of the
>   Student's schedule for editing instead of creating a new one.
> 2a. Course Catalog System does not respond:
>   CES notifies the Student and the use case ends.

Similarly, Step 4 takes several development slices. Since the original extension 4a covered both full course and missing prerequisites, we have to separate those into different extensions, 4a and 4b:

Slices 8 & 9: CES enrolls the Student in the courses, checking prerequisites

> 1. Student requests to construct a schedule. CES prepares a blank schedule form.
> 2. CES gets available courses from the Course Catalog System.
> 3. Student selects up to four primary and two alternate course offerings.
> *4. For each course, CES verifies that the Student has the necessary prerequisites and*
>   *adds the Student to the course, marking the Student as "enrolled" for that course*
>   *in the schedule.*
> 5. The Student indicates the schedule is complete. CES saves it.
> **Extensions:**
> 1a. Student already has a schedule: CES brings up the current version of the
>   Student's schedule for editing instead of creating a new one.
> 2a. Course Catalog System does not respond:
>   CES notifies the Student and the use case ends.
> *4a. Student has not fulfilled all prerequisites:*
>   *CES disables selection of that course and notifies the Student.*
> *(4b. Course full: CES disables selection of that course and notifies the Student.)*

Slice 10: Course full

1. Student requests to construct a schedule. CES prepares a blank schedule form.
2. CES gets available courses from the Course Catalog System.
3. Student selects up to four primary and two alternate course offerings.
4. For each course, CES verifies that the Student has the necessary prerequisites and adds the Student to the course, marking the Student as "enrolled" for that course in the schedule.
5. The Student indicates the schedule is complete. CES saves it.

Extensions:

1a. Student already has a schedule: CES brings up the current version of the Student's schedule for editing instead of creating a new one.
2a. Course Catalog System does not respond:
     CES notifies the Student and the use case ends.
4a. Student has not fulfilled all prerequisites:
     CES disables selection of that course and notifies the Student.
4b. Course full: CES disables selection of that course and notifies the Student.

Slice 11: Semester not in session (completing the use case)

1. Student requests to construct a schedule. CES prepares a blank schedule form.
2. CES gets available courses from the Course Catalog System.
3. Student selects up to four primary and two alternate course offerings.
4. For each course, CES verifies that the Student has the necessary prerequisites and adds the Student to the course, marking the Student as "enrolled" for that course in the schedule.
5. The Student indicates the schedule is complete. CES saves it.

Extensions:

1a. Student already has a schedule: CES brings up the current version of the Student's schedule for editing instead of creating a new one.
1b. Current semester is closed and next semester is not yet open:
     CES lets Student look at existing schedules, but not create new ones.
2a. Course Catalog System does not respond:
     CES notifies the Student and the use case ends.
4a. Student has not fulfilled all prerequisites:
     CES disables selection of that course and notifies the Student.
4b. Course full: CES disables selection of that course and notifies the Student.

This may look preposterously fine-grained to you. However, my purpose in this section is to show you *how* to slice a use case for fine-grained incremental development. You are, of course, welcome to choose fatter slices on your own project. I am showing you my favorite slicing choices to give you a good example to copy.

Fine-grained slicing is valuable because it allows you to develop and test incrementally, to find errors and trouble spots early. Your system will be a lot more complicated than this example. In fact, even part of a step may require a lot of programming – which takes us to **Idea 3**.

Idea 3. Implement just part of a step as its own slice.

Steps 3 and 4 in Register for Courses are good candidates for slicing within a step. They are connected, so we have to take them together. There are several ways to slice, depending on what you like to defer.

If you defer prerequisites validation, you get the following sequence. We start with the *Walking Skeleton* of the business rule:

Slice 5: Add one primary course, without checking prerequisites.
Slice 6: Add up to four primary courses.
Slice 7: Add the two alternatives.
Slice 8: Check prerequisites and handle failure.

Slice 5: Student selects 1 course, CES adds to the schedule, no prerequisites check

> 3. Student selects just one course offering.
> 4. CES adds the Student to the course, marking the Student as "enrolled" for that course in the schedule.

Slice 6: Student adds up to 4 primary courses, still no prerequisites check

> 3. Student selects up to four primary course offerings.
> 4. CES adds the Student to each course, marking the Student as "enrolled" for that course in the schedule.

Slice 7: Student also selects the alternate courses, still no prerequisites check

> 3. Student selects up to four primary and two alternate course offerings.
> 4. CES adds the Student to each course, marking the Student as "enrolled" for that course in the schedule.

Slice 8: Check prerequisites and handle failure

> 3. Student selects up to four primary and two alternate course offerings.
> 4. CES verifies that the Student has the necessary prerequisites for that course, adds the Student to each course, marking the Student as "enrolled" for that course in the schedule.
> **Extensions:**
> 4a. Student has not fulfilled all prerequisites:
>   CES disables selection of that course and notifies the Student.

Personally, I prefer to check the prerequisites earlier – it's "more different" (produces more learning) than just adding another course. That produces the slices (starting from the *Walking Skeleton*):

Slice 5: Add one primary course, without checking prerequisites.

Slice 6: Just one course, but check prerequisites.

> *(Notice we have to handle prerequisites failure right away.)*

Slice 7: Allow up to four primary courses.

Slice 8: Allow the two alternatives.

Slice 5: (Same as before, the Walking Skeleton of the business rule)

> *3. Student selects just one course offering.*
> *4. CES adds the Student to the course, marking the Student as "enrolled" for that course in the schedule.*

Slice 6: Just one course, but check prerequisites, handle prerequisites failure

> 3. Student selects just one course offering.
> 4. CES *verifies that the Student has the necessary prerequisites for that course,* adds the Student to *that* course, marking the Student as "enrolled" for that course in the schedule.
> **Extensions:**
> *4a. Course full or Student has not fulfilled all prerequisites:*
>   *CES disables selection of that course and notifies the Student.*

Slice 7: Add up to 4 primary courses

> 3. Student selects *up to four primary course offerings*.
> 4. CES verifies that the Student has the necessary prerequisites *for the courses*, adds the Student to that course, marking the Student as "enrolled" for that course in the schedule.

Slice 8: Finally, add the alternate courses

> 3. Student selects up to four primary and *two alternate* course offerings.
> 4. CES verifies that the Student has the necessary prerequisites for the courses, adds the Student to that course, marking the Student as "enrolled" for that course in the schedule.

Choose the sequence that suits where you see risks and opportunities.

Idea 4. Some sentences can be done *in different ways*.

This idea is, as far as I know, not generally mentioned in the use case literature. I have taught it, but never wrote it up explicitly until *Unifying User Stories, Use Cases, Story Maps (2024)*.

Let's look at login. The user might log in via email, Google, Facebook or other apps, biometrics, or using a stored cookie.

```
1. User logs in (email, Google, Facebook, biometric, cookie).
```

When the teams are experienced enough, they might not need more than that – they know what to do. Others will want to be explicit. Also, that one step might be delivered in separate deliveries. So we need to find a way to break them out in detail.

My general preference is to list the variations at the end of the use case. That make tracking development easier. Like this:

```
1. User logs in.
2. ....
Step Variations:
1. Log in using:
     Email/password
     Google/Facebook/other app
     Biometric
     Stored cookie
```

Paying for goods is similar:

```
... 7. User pays for items in cart ....
Step Variations:
7. Ways to pay:
     Credit card,
     PayPal,
     bank transfer,
     reward points,
     in installments
```

The following is an example from a real project. (A 'muffin' was the project's name for a web resource.) Here is just one fragment:

VIEW-RATE-COMMENT A MUFFIN !

1. I, a casual viewer, go to Alistair's site and *identify a muffin*.
2. The *server serves up that muffin* (with frostings).
3. I view / scroll / follow links, etc as usual in browsers.
4. I *rate the muffin*.
5. I *add a comment to the discussion about the muffin*.

---

(1) identify a muffin:

(Work Token)	
name its direct URL	11/6/07
name its glossy URL	
name an archaic URL	
via whole-word fragment of the title/body	
via partial-word fragment of the title	
via a major category	2/14
see partial matches in real time as I type	

Seven ways to accomplish the same step! The next page shows more of that same use case.

VIEW-RATE-COMMENT A MUFFIN !

1. I, a casual viewer, go to Alistair's site and *identify a muffin*.
2. The *server serves up that muffin* (with frostings).
3. I view / scroll / follow links, etc as usual in browsers.
4. I *rate the muffin*.
5. I *add a comment to the discussion about the muffin*.

(1) identify a muffin:

(Work Token)	
name its direct URL	11/6/07
name its glossy URL	
name an archaic URL	
via whole-word fragment of the title/body	
via partial-word fragment of the title	
via a major category	2/14
see partial matches in real time as I type	

(2) serve up a muffin:

(Work Token)		
html	11/9/07	PNG
image (gif)	11/9/07	JPG
doc	11/12/07	
YouTube	11/12/07	
pdf	11/13/07	
~~media wiki~~		
textile wiki	11/13/07	
xml		
voice		
PPT	2/2/07	

(2) frostings:

(Work Token)	
comments on the muffin	11/6/07
number of visits to that muffin,	12/14
viewer ratings,	11/14/07
refs to next /prev chronological item,	
refs to next/prev item in top category,	
refs to a couple of purely randomly selected items	
refs to random items within the item's categories	
del.icio.us	
digg.	

As you can see, each step has its own list of variations. The complexity in the system wasn't the use case flow – the whole system consisted of only five or six simple use cases. The complexity lay in all the different ways that each step could be done.

It turned out that we never developed the complete set of any of the steps. You can see that in the dates and the check marks we applied as we went. As we deployed, we saw that many of the things we had thought would be valuable were never actually needed.

In practice, it is quick, fun, and easy to list all the possibilities. You then can decide which to implement now and which to defer. This is particularly important for startups and agile teams.

Idea 5. As with variations of a step, you will also slice your data, your technology variations, complex business rules, performance, and other things.

Here is a short list of the things you might slice up for incremental development;

1. A use case.
2. A subset of a sequence of actions.
3. Various ways to accomplish a single step.
4. Business rules.
5. Data.
6. Technology variations.
7. Interfaces.
8. Performance needs.
9. Risk: Learning how to do it versus actually doing it (see **Idea 6**).

It's not the point of this book to tutor you on how to slice all of those things, although I go into more detail in **Core Concept #4:** *Decompose Everything.*

Idea 6. Split the development into a knowledge-acquisition part and an implementation part.

This is pure project risk management. Imagine you have never connected to a credit card gateway before and are worried that it may be difficult. You have the team program just enough to learn how to do it, and then, knowing that you *can* do it, defer the actual doing until later.

I did that once when converting the data on a site to a new format. I learned that the programmer wasn't comfortable with the assignment and didn't know how to do it. So we split that work into two parts:

1. Learn how to convert the data (early in the project).
2. Actually convert the data (at the end of the project).

You may find yourself in a similar situation where it is useful to split the learning part from the accomplishing part.

Part 4: Perfect your writing: 7 key concepts

What I learned teaching use cases, user stories, and story maps is that no matter what technique you use, you need to master seven core concepts. Master these, and you can use any technique. Make a mess of these, and whatever you write will cause confusion.

These are the key concepts to master:

1.   Manage precision.
2.   Understand how verbs imply durations.
3.   Decompose verbs into shorter-duration verbs.
4.   Decompose everything, not just the verbs.
5.   Write from the user's perspective.
6.   Write just the needs, not the encyclopedia.
7.   Sacrifice perfection for readability.

I end with one bonus concept:

8..   Look for the *Walking Skeleton*.

4.1. Manage precision.

Precision is how much detail you care to mention. Saying a table is "about 2 meters long," or "about 6 feet" is sufficient to organize a room. To manufacture the table, however, you need to know whether it is 2.00 meters plus or minus 0.01, or 6 feet plus or minus ¼".

> *Trivia moment: LEGO blocks are manufactured with tolerances typically around 0.002mm to 0.01mm (2 to 10 micrometers).* [https://medium.com/science-spectrum/the-mind-blowing-engineering-precision-of-lego-ae1aa3a9796c].
> Mind-blowing indeed.

When you start a project, you don't know a lot, so it is easy to say less. Later, when you do know a lot, it is easy to say too much, to provide too much detail, confusing and distracting your readers.

For example, it will distract from your main message if you keep writing about tables that are 0.914 x 1.828 meters instead of 1x2 meters. Although you know the exact number, it's not relevant in most discussions.

This concept of precision applies to all work products you will ever produce. It applies equally to your strategic roadmap, performance requirements, security, data needs, interface definitions, user interface, in fact, everything.

Manage your use of precision, both when you don't yet have the information, and also after you have it. Restrain yourself from mentioning everything.

Here are examples in low, high, and super-high precision:

For a use case:

Low precision: Just the title

> Buy candy

High precision: The title, main success scenario, extensions.

> Buy Candy
> **Main success scenario:**
> 1. Customer selects candy. Machine shows price and allows money to be put in.
> 2. Customer puts in the money.
> 3. Machine drops the candy and the change.
> **Extensions:**
> 1a. No more of that candy:
>   Machine shows "Empty" and doesn't accept money.
> 1b. No change available in the machine:
>   Machine puts up "Exact change required".
> 3a. No change available in the machine:
>   Machine drops the candy but not the change.

Super high precision: All the test cases

> (Imagine here the series of test cases needed to test all variations of those scenarios)

For data:

Low precision: Just the nickname

```
Customer information
```

or perhaps

```
Customer name, address, phone number, etc.
```

High precision: The fields named

```
Customer name:
    First name, Middle initial, Last name
Address:
    Street number and name
    City, State, Zip Code
Phone number:
    Area code + 7-digit number
```

Super high precision: The validation requirements on the data

```
Customer name:
    First name: alphanumeric, truncate at 22 chars
    (etc.)
Address:
    9-digit U.S. zip code
    (etc.)
```

I hope you can see from these examples that if you are passing your work around to a wide variety of readers, you need to pay attention to what level of precision they need to see.

4.2. Understand that verbs imply durations.

All verbs take time. Surprisingly, people seem to have a similar sense of time needed for most verbs.

- When you write "get cash from an ATM," you already have in mind that that will take 2-5 minutes.
- When you write "manage my investment portfolio," you and your reader both know it is an activity that goes for years.
- "Put on my socks" is probably less than a minute.
- "Select a quantity" should take a few seconds, not several minutes.

Interestingly, people around the world commonly seem to feel that an ordinary user task might take between two and 20 minutes. That covers ordinary activities like "Buy a <something>," "Fill the car with gas," "Update my profile," and so on.

Experienced readers will recognize that these actions map to database transactions or atomic business processes.

Most people don't consciously think about the time implied by each verb while they are writing. They mix them up all over the place, putting a few-second verb next to a 20-minute or months-long verb.

Readers sense the imbalance. When the verbs don't tell a sensible story, they feel uncomfortable, they get confused, implement things wrong, and make mistakes.

To fix this, use the *altitude* metaphor. Verbs that take more time are *higher*, verbs that take less time are *lower*.

Tag that globally understood 2-20 minute user task or atomic business process as being at *sea level*. Then all the longer timelines naturally go above it ("kite level" to "cloud level"), and all the shorter timelines naturally go below it ("fish level" to "clam level").

Kite-level verbs (and use cases) are great for describing long-running activities or macro-processes. Sea-level verbs are great for describing what people want to accomplish in a single sitting or single visit.

Fish-level verbs are great for giving blow-by-blow, second by second instructions.

Clam-level verbs also show blow-by-blow actions, but should never be expanded to become their own use cases.

For example, "Insert card into ATM" names a goal that takes time, and has steps and failure modes. It fulfills all the requirements for a use case. However, you will probably never want to write and track that use case separately. It's a clam.

Use the altitude metaphor to write verbs at consistent levels on purpose. Your teams have less confusion and your systems have fewer holes when you do this.

Once you learn to do this, you can write use cases, scenarios, user stories, story maps, epics, whatever you like, in ways that tell an easy-to-understand story, without generating confusion. Your reader will just read and follow along.

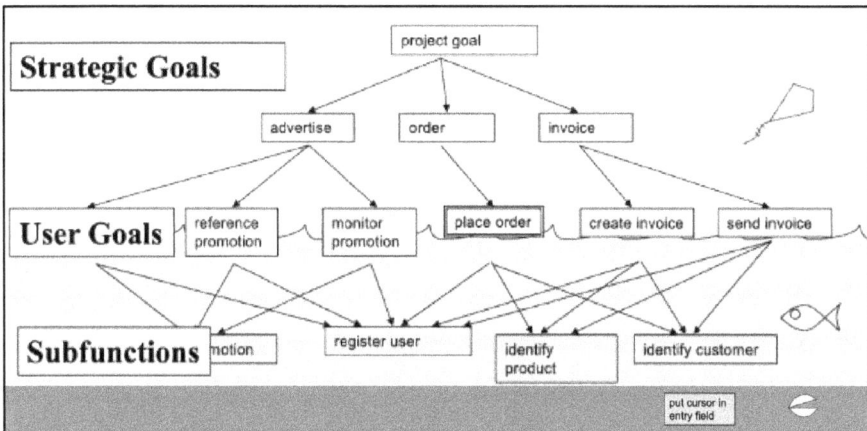

Figure 4.2-1. Sea level, kite level, fish, clam level goals.

4.3. Decompose verbs into shorter-duration verbs.

Goals have subgoals. To reach a goal, one must succeed at all the subgoals. Suppose you want to *"Win a major client."* You break it down into subgoals:

- Get a list of top clients.
- Choose one to approach.
- Take that person to lunch.
- ... etc....

"Get a list of top clients" might involve talking to people, researching on the internet, getting their contact information, and so on.

"Take that person to lunch" also has steps: design an invitation, contact them, invite them, make a table reservation, go to the restaurant, etc.

"Eat lunch" breaks into order food, eat soup, eat the main, and so on.

"Eat soup" breaks into *"Eat one spoonful,"* which breaks into lift spoon, put spoon into soup, etc.

This breaking down of verbs never ends. Actions break into sub-actions down to the quantum properties of time. At some point, of course, you'll stop.

Going down the ladder is fairly obvious - Ask:

> *"How does one do that?"*

You will answer that question using lower-level verbs.

Going *up* the ladder is less obvious. The opposite of *How?* is *Why?* However, there are many flavors of *why*. "Because it makes me happy" doesn't get us the higher-level verb. So we ask:

> *"In order to accomplish what?"*

Or just

> *"In order to what?"*

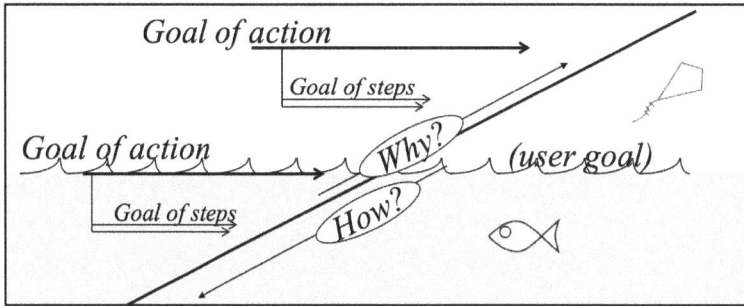

Figure 4-3-1. Sea level, kite level, fish level goals nest.

For example:

- You put the spoon in the soup in order to what?
- In order to eat the soup. You did that in order to what?
- As part of eating the meal. And you were eating the meal, why? In order to accomplish what?
- To soften up this potential client.
- And why did you do that? In order to accomplish what?
- In order to sell my services.

And so on.

Good writing hinges on balancing verb levels, breaking them down as needed and rolling them up as needed. Most people don't think about verbs having implicit timelines, so they don't notice they are mixing verb levels and confusing their audience. Use the altitude metaphor to help tune your writing.

Before closing, I should mention one trap in trying to break down verbs into verbs of shorter duration: People automatically tend to peek *inside* the system being designed to answer the question.

This is wrong.

Imagine I ask you to break down "Customer validates self with an ATM card." Odds are that, especially if you are an engineer, you will immediately start describing the insides of the ATM.

Don't do that. You are writing this use case to describe what will be designed by someone else. You are not doing the design here. It is the designer's job to do the actual design. You won't get it right, and they'll be mad at you.

Shrink the time duration of the verb but stay outside the system.

4.4. Decompose everything, not just the verbs.

Almost everything can be developed incrementally and deployed at just a fraction of its full version. You don't need all of the user interface design, the external technologies, performance, security, etc.

Therefore, identify the smallest subset of the data needed to advance the system design. Look for the smallest UX path that allows you to get feedback. Look for the myriad ways that people accomplish what looks like a simple verb.

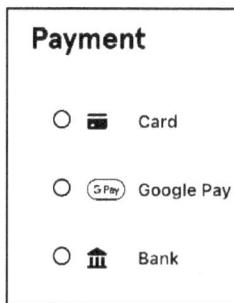

Figure 4-4-1. Various payment methods.

For example, you don't need to develop your system with all payment methods at one time. Choose whichever is simplest for your first increment. When the time is right, choose another.

You probably don't need to process payments split across different credit cards to start with, either.

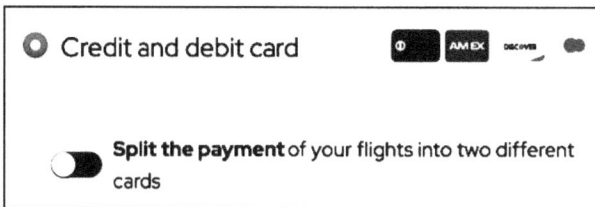

Figure 4-4-2. Splitting a payment across cards.

The same goes with the data. To get the user profile page working, you don't need the name, address, email, phone, security information, personal preferences, and reward status.

Get your first slice working with just the last name and nothing else. That will force you to connect to the database, show things on the screen and create the profile viewing and editing pages.

Start by getting the *Walking Skeleton* running.

From there, add more columns to the database, more data elements on the screen, and so on.

If you don't decompose all these other things, you will have fat development slices, which means slow development, slow feedback, latent errors, late delivery, and features that never get used.

4.5. Write from the user's perspective.

Think of a store manager walking around throughout their day. At various points, that person will turn to the computer to accomplish some task on their work list. It could be to check for out-of-stock items, produce the daily rollup, or track sales results. These are the needs and wants of a person doing their job.

Not only programmers, but even many business analysts have a hard time putting themselves in the user's eyes and seeing the world from their standpoint. Instead, they stand inside the system, looking out from inside the box, as it were.

Here's a common error:

```
Get cash
System: ATM        Primary actor: Customer        Goal Level: Sea
Main success scenario:
   1. Accept card.
   2. Accept PIN. Validate PIN.
   3. Accept amount. Check balance.
   4. Dispense cash, update balance.
```

To the programmer writing this, all of this is obvious. They are providing a service to the user and describing what they will program.

However, use cases are to be read by everyone in the organization, from executives to the training team. Their main value is aligning the organization on what's being built. Having dozens of use cases written that way pretty much guarantees that they won't get read, the organization won't know what's getting built, and there will be a lot of surprises (read: mistakes) in what gets delivered.

Imagine asking your user base and the executives: "Is this the system you want? Will this fit into your life and make your life easier?"

What you are after is, "Yes, this is what we want/need, and yes, this is everything, with no critical holes," or just as valuable, "No, this isn't what we want. It's wrong here..." Those are the only people who can answer those questions, so the use cases have to be readable to them.

Here's what happens when you write from the user's perspective:

The user experience team watched some users' working with their word-processing system. They kept seeing people spending time on very small changes in line spacing, font size and so on.

They asked the users why they were doing all these things ("In order to accomplish what?"). It turned out that the users were fussing with those details to avoid having just a little bit of text flow over onto the next page.

So they offered a "Make this fit on one page" button, which made minor changes to line spacing and font sizes to avoid the page break.

(I don't know where that feature went – I've been wanting it nonstop while writing this book!)

To close out this section, here is a lovely little usage story for an ATM that one of my students wrote, with a twist I never would have expected:

Jenny wakes up at 3 a.m. with her withdrawal kicking in. She desperately needs her fix. She jumps into her Benz convertible and texts the ATM. Slowing down as she pulls through the bank, the ATM lobs a paper bag with $2,000 in small bills into her convertible, she drives off to score her fix.

I'll bet you wouldn't have come up with *those* requirements just writing from inside the box! And you won't be surprised to learn that this was written in San Francisco :).

4.6. Write just the needs, not the encyclopedia.

The top value of use cases is keeping the entire organization aligned. That means everyone needs to be comfortable reading them. That means not putting everything you know into them.

A good use case is typically half a page long, maybe a page. Only a few ever take two pages to cover all the alternatives. They are all easy to read.

The problem is they are too useful for their own good: The list of use cases provides a superb index into the system. People therefore quite naturally start putting all the extra information needed to develop the system *right into the use case*. They include details needed by the UX designers, database designers, programmers, and testers.

Oops. Just destroyed the readability. That means people won't read them, which means you just lost their top value.

The answer is to put that information, the encyclopedia, into side documents and link them. That allows the people who need the details to get them while keeping the use cases themselves readable.

4.7. Sacrifice perfection for readability.

Casual use cases will get read. Hard-to-read use cases won't.

I can teach you to write the perfect use case. However, it became clear to me at some point that diminishing returns set in very early with use cases.

Casual use cases are incomplete. They are unlikely to cover all the extension conditions. However, they are quick to write and easy to read, and therefore easy to pass around the organization, providing the top value to the organization.

On my first big project, we wrote 240 use cases in casual style, omitting many extension conditions. They were used as the basis for a ten-million-dollar contract, examined at the beginning for completeness and at the end for conformance. They were sufficient to their purpose.

Personally, I write use cases in the style with the line numbers. It keeps me on track and lets me poke for holes. At the same time, I work really hard to keep them easy to read, even twisting the format as needed to fit the readership.

For example, in use case 6, *+Manage Asset*, I used the concrete narrative style with line numbering, so that anyone in this large organization could see their overall business process. The use case goes for several pages, as it covers all the field assets they manage, from birth to death. I played with alliteration in the names and anything else I could come up with to make them readable and reasonably complete.

The end of the story is this: Approximate use cases get read. If they are easy to read, your reader will understand what they are building, and maybe find a problem. And that's what you want.

4.8. *Bonus tip:* Find the *Walking Skeleton.*

A Walking Skeleton is a tiny implementation of a process or system that allows a small end-to-end function.

I ran into this concept in the 1990s when a senior designer showed me how they safely evolved a difficult technical architecture because they started with a completely trivial initial implementation and evolved it from there to its final design. I had the opportunity to put this idea in practice on my next project and saw how well it worked.

Jeff Patton uses it to describe deploying a system in stages, starting from the smallest set of functions that cross multiple users, delivering a very thin but noticeable value to the organization. This is in contrast to deploying a lot of functions to just one user group, in which case the organization doesn't benefit from the new system.

In the case of the RFID project (Chapter 3.2), they were able to get direct business benefit from delivering their technical *Walking Skeleton.*

The *Walking Skeleton* concept is a great strategy for incremental development and staged deployment, allowing you to reduce risk and gain business value early.

- Deliver the *Walking Skeleton* of a business process to get early value from the system and early feedback on its use.
- Implement the *Walking Skeleton* of a use case to show progress and get feedback early;
- Implement the *Walking Skeleton* of a complex business rule for the same reason;
- Design and build the *Walking Skeleton* of your technical architecture to discover technical issues early and allow parallel evolution of the design;

Read more about it online:

[https://web.archive.org/web/20140329201356/http://alistair.cockburn.us/Walking+skeleton]

Fin

Read the complete definition of use cases in *"Writing Effective Use Cases."* See their relation to user stories and story maps in *"Unifying user stories, use cases, story maps."*

For the rest, I send you my best wishes with your writing and collaborating.

Alistair

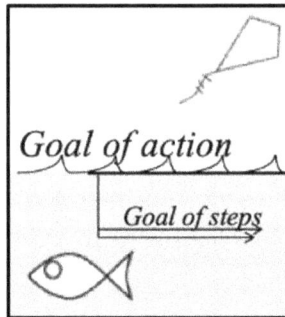

About the Author

Dr. Alistair Cockburn (pronounced CO-BURN), known for his wild hair photo, was named as one of the "42 Greatest Software Professionals of All Times" in 2020, as a world expert on project management, software architecture, use cases, and agile development.

Besides co-authoring the Agile Manifesto, he wrote the award-winning books *Writing Effective Use Cases* and *Agile Software Development: The Cooperative Game*.

In 2015, he created the *Heart of Agile* concept to be used in every kind of initiative, including social impact projects, governments, and families. For his latest work, see https://alistaircockburn.com/

He is most likely to show up in your workshop looking like this.

Books by Alistair Cockburn

Surviving Object Oriented Projects	1997
Writing Effective Use Cases	2000
Agile Software Development (1st ed)	2001
Patterns for Effective Use Cases	2002
People and Methodologies in Software Development (Dr. Philos. dissertation)	2003
Crystal Clear: A human-powered methodology for small teams	2004
Agile Software Development: The cooperative game (2nd ed)	2006
Design in Object Technology: Class of 1994	2021
Design in Object Technology: The Annotated Class of 1994	2022
Love Trio Trio del Amor (selected poems)	2022
Unifying User Stories, Use Cases, Story Maps	2024
Hexagonal Architecture Explained	2024
The Mini-Book on Use Cases	2025

See the full list at https://alistaircockburn.com/Books

www.ingramcontent.com/pod-product-compliance
Lightning Source LLC
Chambersburg PA
CBHW040908210326
41597CB00029B/5010